# GOVTECH

## Elevating City and Tech Park Competitiveness

## Stephan S. Sunn

**Davidson Global Partners, LLC**

Copyright © 2024 Stephan S. Sunn

©Copyright 2024 -2026 Stephan Sun All Rights Reserved

Disclaimer:

This book may not be reproduced or transmitted in any form without the written permission of the authors. Every effort has been made to make this guide as complete and accurate as possible. Although the authors have prepared this guide with the greatest of care, and have made every effort to ensure its accuracy, we assume no responsibility or liability for errors, inaccuracies, or omissions. Before you begin, check with the appropriate authorities to ensure compliance with all laws and regulations. Every effort has been made to make this report as complete and accurate as possible. However, there may be mistakes in typography or content. Also, this report contains information on online marketing and technology only up to the publishing date. Therefore, this report should be used as a guide – not as the ultimate source of Internet marketing information. The purpose of this report is to educate. The authors do not warrant that the information contained in this report is fully complete and shall not be responsible for any errors or omissions. The authors shall have neither liability nor responsibility to any person or entity concerning any loss or damage caused or alleged to be caused directly or indirectly by this report, nor do we make any claims or promises of our ability to generate income by using any of this information.

Davidson Global Partners & Co. LLC, Davidson, NC 28036, USA; All Inquiries of copyrights, and cooperation go to: Stephan.sunn@aya.yale.edu

# CONTENTS

Title Page
Copyright
Preface
Chapter 1: GovTech Reshapes Governments
Chapter 2: Building a GovTech Ecosystem
Chapter 3: GovTech for Business Growth
Chapter 4: Transforming Key Government Functions
Chapter 5: The Human Factor in GovTech Adoption
Chapter 6: Financing GovTech
Chapter 7: Smart Cities and Urban Governance
Chapter 8: Public-Private Partnerships and Innovations
Chapter 9: Cybersecurity and Data Privacy in GovTech
Chapter 10: Measuring Success of GovTech Programs
Chapter 11: Emerging Trends and Long-Term Vision
Chapter 12: Examples of GovTech Implementations
Acknowledgement
About The Author
Books By This Author

# PREFACE

The author and his partners contributing to this series of professional guidance and industry best practices possess over two decades of experience advising multinational corporations and C-suite executives. They are esteemed thought leaders within their respective fields and globally renowned throughout their extensive professional networks. Prior to the COVID-19 pandemic, when international travel was unencumbered, they would convene annually at a rotating global location. Their first reunion following that worldwide crisis was imbued with a profound sense of gratitude for having endured such a cataclysmic event.

Reuniting with one another brought joy to all of us. Even more so, the notion of how delicate and short life began to settle in. The idea of documenting our business experience and lessons, successes or failures, to help our colleagues and clients was formed in 2022 when we gathered in Jamaica. However, with the arrival of ChatGPT and similar trailblazing AI technologies in late 2022, this small proposal gains urgency because we fear within the next decade these revolutionary technologies could transform our lives and society forever, and resemble what COVID-19 has brought to us.

The subject matter of this book series are the business domains we have supported clients worldwide last two decades, with the priority in the last few years. We don't claim we are the researchers or professors in the technologies, but the practitioners who evaluate, choose, and apply state-of-the-art technologies to solve business problems. The technology breakthroughs are not what we pursued, the critical criterion is if the technology solved the business problems with business values. This is why "Case Studies", "Examples" or "Lessons" are weighted much higher than the rigorous analytics of the theories in these business guides.

This book dives into GovTech's potential to revolutionize government and urban development. By leveraging data, AI, and e-government platforms, GovTech can streamline processes, boost transparency, and even enhance citizen engagement. The book emphasizes collaboration between government, businesses, academia, and citizens to create a thriving GovTech ecosystem. Success stories from Estonia and Singapore showcase how GovTech can attract investment, streamline business operations, and fuel economic growth.

Furthermore, the book explores GovTech's role in fostering innovation hubs and simplifying business registrations, particularly for SMEs. It also delves into the power of data-driven governance and AI to transform public services and policymaking. Finally, the human aspect is crucial. Building a skilled workforce, managing cultural shifts, and promoting digital literacy are all emphasized for GovTech to reach its full potential.

# CHAPTER 1: GOVTECH RESHAPES GOVERNMENTS

Transforming Government for the 21st Century

Almost every facet of our existence has been revised by the fast speed of technology, from how we correspond with co-workers to how we obtain services to how we link with the globe. However, society all too often outstrips government, catching ill-trained, unprepared governments entirely off guard. We have a laundry list of woes from traditional governmental organizations. They are unproductive. They're arthritic. They're insensitive. They're uninformed.

In the modern era of digitalization, people anticipate public services to be as helpful, accessible, and user-friendly as the services private businesses provide. They want to be able to locate information, fill out forms, and engage with their representatives from behind their computer screens, without having to move through bureaucratic thickets or carve time from a busy day to wait on line. Businesspeople, too, require ease in registering their company, securing a license or permit, or adhering to rules.

Fortunately, there's a new wave of innovation moving to tackle these challenges and reimagine government for the 21st century, known as GovTech. This innovation holds the potential to change the way in which governments work, deliver services, and engage their citizens.

At its heart, GovTech involves using technology to make government work better. This can be seen in various ways. It could be cutting down on repetitive jobs and doing processes more efficiently, using data analytics and artificial intelligence for decision-making and resource allocation, or it could be as simple as making services faster and easier to use. By adopting these technologies, governments can save money, offer better services, and keep citizens happy.

One big benefit of GovTech is how it can make governments more transparent and accountable. By making government information and services accessible online through e-government platforms and open data initiatives, GovTech can let people see where their taxes go, follow what's happening with public works projects, and then hold their elected officials accountable for results. Greater accountability can help build trust between people and their government, stimulating more civic participation and democratic activity.

Another potential benefit of GovTech, of course, is the way it could transform the way citizens interact with their government. Enabled to provide feedback, submit ideas, and participate in decision-making processes through virtual town hall tools. Conducting polls and surveys online is cheaper and more efficient, and using social media to crowdsource ideas, for example, can mean hearing from voices and perspectives that might not normally be heard – or that might not be comfortable speaking up in person. The endgame here is that by getting more people who care about a given outcome involved, outcomes are more likely to be what citizens need and want.

All around the world, governments are in the process of recognizing the potential of GovTech. More and more countries are investing into digital infrastructure, developing innovation applications, and partnering with the private to drive growth and innovation. Whether it's Estonia's world-leading e-government platform or Singapore's smart city initiative, these global case studies demonstrate the myriad applications and benefits of GovTech across sectors.

In the 21st century, the need for governments to rate GovTech will only increase. As technology evolves rapidly and consumers and businesses make more demands on governments, governments that fail to adapt risk falling behind and losing the confidence and confidence of the people they represent. Through the positive adoption of GovTech, however, governments can take the lead in driving technology and communicating better with their constituents.

In the forthcoming chapters, focus will be on core building blocks for a thriving GovTech ecosystem including engagement with stakeholders, development of innovative applications, creation of entrepreneurship responses, capitalization of the human factor, and ensuring security and privacy of citizen data. By sharing real-time insights, case studies, and expert opinions, the book will explain and guide government leaders and stakeholders on how to pathways with GovTech approach for better, efficient and effective service delivery.

# CHAPTER 2: BUILDING A GOVTECH ECOSYSTEM

To successfully develop and implement GovTech initiatives, numerous actors have to actively participate and cooperate. Those actors bring along various know-how, expertise, and resources, hence giving birth to a strong and resilient GovTech ecosystem. We will turn our focus to those key players in the development of a powerful GovTech landscape and highlight the crucial significance of their interaction.

Strong government leadership and a clear vision for technology adoption are vital features of any GovTech ecosystem. National and regional government officials have to acknowledge the transformative potential of GovTech and be its champion. This entails creating dedicated government agencies or units that lead GovTech initiatives, set strategic goals, and allocate resources. These agencies drive GovTech adoption, ensuring it aligns with national priorities and instilling a culture of innovation across government.

Nonetheless, governments cannot set up a GovTech infrastructure on their own. The private sector has a cardinal role to play in crafting and implementing pioneering solutions. Tech businesses, start-ups, and entrepreneurs bring cutting-edge knowledge, nimbleness, and citizen-centered designs to the table. Governments need to work with the private sector proactively through various collaboration models, for example, public-private partnerships (PPPs) as well as innovation challenges. PPPs let governments exploit the technical capacities and resources of private firms, thus guaranteeing they dovetail with public sector goals and requirements. Innovation challenges, like hackathons and pilot schemes, afford start-ups and entrepreneurs opportunities to demonstrate their ideas and win government contracts.

To ensure governments and the private sector work together effectively, there needs to be clear rules of the game, standards, and a carrot and stick. It means creating an environment where the private sector can participate, bureaucratic form-filling is reduced, and the procurement process is fair and transparent. That may include tweaking regulations, providing tax incentives, or setting up funding streams specifically for GovTech start-ups.

By creating an environment conducive to involvement by the private sector governments hope to tap not just into money, but into ideas, entrepreneurialism and problem-solving nous.

The ecosystem of GovTech crucially includes academia and civil society organizations. These actors are rich in knowledge, expertise and understanding of the citizen's needs and concerns. Civil society organizations encompass advocacy groups and community-based organizations. They are equipped to amplify the voice of the excluded and vulnerable, ensuring that GovTech initiatives are inclusive, accessible and responsive to the diverse populations that government is serving. These organizations can also be bridges between governments and citizens. They play a key role in raising public awareness and encouraging citizens to participate GovTech's programs.

Academic organizations, including universities and research institutes, are vital constituents of the GovTech system. They are engaged in investigation, they are creators of new technologies, and they often provide special courses and training. They are uniquely positioned to provide government stakeholders with the latest information, to recommend leading behaviors, and to develop the skills and competencies that public sector employees require. When governments and their academic companions work together, transformative innovations may come to pass. Data sharing, resource allocation methods, and effectiveness frameworks are instances of tasks that the government and academia might jointly undertake in the GovTech domain. These teams also may help guarantee the highest levels of public services. Because the GovTech industry depends upon an apt, agile workforce, and because experts in the sector are typically graduated from colleges and universities, collaboration with these knowledge providers is a must.

Establishing clear governance structures and collaboration mechanisms among stakeholders is critical for the success of GovTech initiatives. This may involve the establishment of multi-stakeholder forums, working groups, or advisory committees that include representatives from government, the private sector, civil society, and academia. These platforms enable discussion, the exchange of knowledge, and solutions co-creation. This makes sure that GovTech initiatives stay well-coordinated, that they are consistent with common objectives, and that they align with the needs of all stakeholders.

To summarize what we presented in this chapter, the creation of a flourishing GovTech ecosystem necessitates the participation and united effort of various actors in a region: government authorities, civil society organizations, the private sector and academic establishments. Through availing the strengths and know-how of these interconnected groups, governments can pave the way for original ideas, tailor-made services and digitalized public services. These will be tackled in subsequent chapters based on practical experience, exemplary cases and achievements.

# CHAPTER 3: GOVTECH FOR BUSINESS GROWTH

In today's highly competitive world economy, governments are increasingly looking to GovTech as a means of driving economic development and fostering business growth. By exploiting digital technologies and innovative solutions, governments can create the conditions for entrepreneurship, attract investment, and nurture sectors of the economy that are critical to growth. This chapter considers how GovTech can be applied to streamline business processes, provide direct support to businesses, and consequently underpin prosperity.

There are various ways that GovTech can help grow the economy, but of all of them, one of the main ones is by making business registration and licensing faster and simpler. Historically, setting up a business or getting the licenses and permits needed to start a specific business has been a slow and painful process full of bureaucracy and multiple government agencies. By digitizing these procedures and producing online platforms for business registration and licensing, economies can reduce the administrative burden businesses must confront. This saves entrepreneurs' time and money, promotes the formalization of businesses, increases tax revenue and boosts job creation.

Take, for example, the Estonian government. They have been one of the first to implement a completely online process for registering businesses, via their e-Business Register. Entrepreneurs can register their businesses online in a matter of minutes, completely devoid of physical paperwork or a trip to the government office. This simplicity is a large reason why Estonia has earned its name as one of the most startup and business-friendly countries in the world. This has even started to gain them a large amount of foreign investments.

Besides making administrative enforcement easier, GovTech can also provide SMEs and start-ups with precious tools and resources. A government can develop digital platforms providing a range of services, such as information about funding opportunities, mentorship programs, market intelligence, and so on. With this way, businesses can easily run on the complex map of government support as well as they can easily connect to, and access resources, and networks that they need because they are relevant to them.

For example, the Singaporean administration has created a complete and inclusive online door named "GoBusiness", where companies can find and get to know all the government services and sources they need. The door contains a package of tools, including "Grants and Assistance" for business and service finders, licensing as well as regulatory advisory and finally the guide. His resources are granted centrally and used amicably by the government, with the purpose of granting the growth and competitive ability of small-medium businesses and startups in Singapore.

Another important role for GovTech is in attracting investment and driving innovation in key industries. The government can use digital technology to build smart cities and innovation districts across the country, providing the perfect environment for businesses to grow. By investing in digital foundations, such as high-speed broadband networks and Internet of Things (IoT) sensors, the government can create the right conditions for entrepreneurs and technology companies alike to set up shop.

Dubai has aggressively pursued a smart city agenda, with ventures like the Dubai Smart City Accelerator and the Dubai Future Accelerators programs being implemented. The focus of these programs is to lure novel startups to the emirate and collaborate on developing technologies for the city. Urban challenges such as healthcare, energy and transportation are among the issues that the startups will need to focus on in their development of new technologies. Moreover, by gaining a reputation as an innovation hub and supplying the right conditions for growth, Dubai has successfully drawn in major investments and also cultivated a booming technology sector.

Furthermore, GovTech can be used to foster specific businesses and industries that are important to economic improvement. Governments can use online apps to facilitate the promotion of trade and exports, linking regional companies with global markets. With big data and artificial intelligence, they can monitor what is developing and upcoming in important sectors, such as tourism, agriculture and manufacturing, and enact targeted measures to help these businesses flourish.

In summary, GovTech offers huge opportunities for economic growth and business development. By improving business processes, supporting SMEs and startups with critical resources, attracting investment, and boosting innovation in priority sectors, governments can create a business friendly environment that supports growth. With the rise of the digital economy and more intense global competition, it is clear that GovTech is key to unlocking new drivers of economic growth and job creation for those governments that embrace this change. In the following chapters we will see examples of GovTech in action, and indicators of best practice from across the world.

# CHAPTER 4: TRANSFORMING KEY GOVERNMENT FUNCTIONS

The use of GovTech has the potential to revolutionize segments of government operations creating more efficient, transparent, and citizen-centric processes. This chapter explores three core GovTech applications that are revamping critical government functions, namely: e-government services; data-driven governance; and the use of artificial intelligence in government.

E-government services are one of the most visible manifestations of GovTech. E-government involves the use of digital technologies to deliver public services to citizens and businesses online. These include services such as license renewals, permit applications, tax filing, and benefit claims. By offering these services through online platforms, governments can dramatically cut the administrative burden on citizens and businesses, saving them both time and effort.

In order for e-government efforts to be successful, governments need to prioritize user-centered design and accessibility. The online platforms should require no advanced knowledge of how to use the internet, be easy to maneuver, and it would be accessible to all citizens, including those with disabilities. In addition to this, the government must invest in systems that can be used safely for payment gateways and secure ideas to enable transactions to be safe and while maintaining online privacy.

With over 99% of public services available online, Estonia is a global leader in e-government services. All these services are accessed through one platform, e-Estonia. It supports digital access to almost the entire gamut of government services from voting and health care to education and business registration, using a single digital identity. Not only has this greatly increased the efficiency of governmental services, but it has also greatly increased transparency and trust in public institutions.

Another major application of GovTech is data-driven governance, built on the premise that governments generate and collect vast amounts of data through a variety of sources, such as census surveys, administrative records, and sensor networks. By leveraging this data, governments can generate valuable insights into public needs, optimize resource allocation, and inform evidence-based policymaking.

On the other hand, using data in governance raises significant concerns about privacy and security. Governments must build strong data governance frameworks that guarantee that citizen data is collected, stored, and utilized responsibly. This includes imposing rigid access controls, anonymization techniques, and disclosure practices to respect the privacy rights of the citizens.

With programs such as the Mayor's Office of Data Analytics, the city of New York has been a leader in data-driven governance. The Mayor's Office of Data Analytics is able to use data to solve problems and improve service delivery across all agencies in one of the most complex cities in the world. Since 2012, the Mayor's Office of Data Analytics has continued a concentrated focus on how analytics can be used as a tool for change. Through delivery-focused pilots and long-term projects, the Mayor's Office of Data Analytics has continued to validate the role of data in driving the City forward. They have identified buildings with the risk of fires, have been able to assign ambulances more efficiently, and have been able to test seventy potential health interventions to identify the best programs in a high-need neighborhood.

Last but not least, AI is rising as a potent tool for reshaping the operations of the government. There is a plethora of applications for AI to make our government more effective, from 24/7 chatbot helpdesks to predictive analytics aiming to eliminate waste and fraud. It's not just about creating a chatbot or whatever. It's building the capability for continuous and rapid improvement after the initial deployment. It comes down to organizational agility and how organizations learn from data. Additionally, AI can help agencies automate repetitive tasks, such as document processing, data entry and other tedious jobs, freeing up employees to focus on more important tasks

Artificial intelligence (AI) has great potential in the field of public safety and emergency management. By collecting data from various sources, such as security cameras, social media, and weather sensors, AI systems can detect potential incidents and optimize response efforts in real-time. For instance, The city of New Orleans is teaming up with Veris for the creation of an AI system that anticipates where and how likely a car wreck will be, optimally allocating responses as time goes on.

There are significant upsides to artificial intelligence (AI), but also critical ethical and social considerations. Governments must ensure AI systems are transparent, accountable, and unbiased. They must also engage in public dialogue and stakeholder consultation to ensure AI deployment in government is consistent with societal values and preferences.

To conclude, the three GovTech applications of e-government services, data-driven governance, and AI are transforming core government functions. Using these technologies, governments make public services more effective and efficient, create better-informed policies, and have a positive impact on citizens' lives. Delivering GovTech though requires addressing privacy, security, and ethical considerations. The remaining chapters will examine the human and organizational dimensions of GovTech adoption. We will look at the need to build digital skills, to manage change as digital tools come into use, and fund new, innovative approaches.

# CHAPTER 5: THE HUMAN FACTOR IN GOVTECH ADOPTION

Although technology is central to GovTech, its successful implementation and uptake hinges on the human element. Governments must invest in developing the requisite skills, knowledge, and mindsets among their personnel to make effective use of digital technologies for public service provision. This chapter looks at three critical facets of building GovTech capacity: creating a skilled GovTech workforce; managing change and cultural transformation; and promoting citizen digital literacy.

In the digital era, governments face a significant issue: a limited supply of professionals specialized in designing, executing, and administering GovTech solutions. Most government employees lack the necessary digital competencies and skills to function with up-and-coming concepts, such as AI, blockchain, and IoT. Governments need to invest in comprehensive capacity-building programs, which focus on transferring knowledge and competencies to employees, to eliminate this gap.

This could entail a wide array of efforts, such as internal educational plans, alliances with learning institutions, or transfers with non-governmental businesses. Singapore, for instance, has rolled out the GovTech Talent Program, a scholarship and internship program designed to heighten the influx of technical skills within the public sector. The plan offers training in areas involving cybersecurity, data science, and software engineering, alongside attempts at building exposure to real-world ventures and mentorship.

In addition to technical skills, building capacity in GovTech also involves nurturing soft skills that include problem-solving, collaboration, and creativity. Governments need to foster a culture of innovation and experimentation, encouraging employees to take risks and adopt new ways of working. This may involve changes to traditional hierarchical structures and decision-making processes, as well as the embracing of agile and user-centered design methodologies.

Nevertheless, what this truly means is that developing a GovTech staff that is competent in the public sector is just one half of the solution; you also need to create an administration that is able to cope with the changes in culture and organization that will be brought on by the digitization of citizens' interactions with government. Since government agencies are infamously top-heavy and encrusted with legacy systems, there is likely to be substantial resistance to this effort. Overcoming such resistance will require leadership that is and will persist in being stronger than the forces of inertia arrayed against it; constant, consistent messaging; and a great deal of small wins that add up to the big wins.

Tailored change management strategies are necessary, designing interventions that match the unique needs and contextual requirements of an organization or agency. Interventions can range from redesigning processes and employee engagement initiatives to leadership development programs. The agency's unique needs and its primary workforce demographics, its organizational culture are a few examples of factors that should be considered when selecting a change strategy.

Demonstrating that governments can execute cultural transformation in the digital environment, the United States Digital Service (USDS) is a new model. It's a team of designers and technologists in the federal government, founded in 2014 to help make public services work better for everyone. Working like a startup, the team advocates for user-centered design, agile development, and continuous delivery. By helping to embed those practices in federal government agencies, they drive cultural change and build digital capacity throughout the federal government.

In conclusion, GovTech capacity-building also needs to prioritize digital literacy for citizens. As more government services begin to operate online, it becomes vital that all citizens possess the skills, knowledge, and ability to navigate and utilize these services. This is doubly important for marginalized communities and groups who face barriers to digital inclusion: limited access to devices or connectivity, for example.

Digital literacy can be supported by various government interventions such as public awareness campaigns, community-driven training programs, and partnerships with civil society organizations. For example, the United Kingdom (UK) government has developed the Digital Inclusion Strategy which aims to make sure everyone has the skills and confidence they need to use digital technologies. The strategy is made up of a set of initiatives, including the Future Digital Inclusion program which provides community-based or local digital skills training to selected groups who are under-served by existing provisions, and the Digital Skills Partnership which is a cross-sector initiative that brings together government, industry, charities and voluntary organizations to promote digital inclusion.

To sum up, the development of GovTech can only be completed if we consider the human sides included in adopting technology. The aspects that human sides related to how to use GovTech, include workforce skills, change management within an organization, and digital literacy knowledge of citizens. If we need GovTech service to be really beneficial and functional, the government should concentrate on developing these mentioned factors that we call enzymes. This chapter mentioned about value of partnerships to drive GovTech, and of course data privacy and cybersecurity, the two most important factors to show the rightness and full trust in GovTech.

# CHAPTER 6: FINANCING GOVTECH

Innovative Funding Models for Sustainable Growth

Funding of GovTech initiatives is a crucial challenge for governments globally. The advantages of GovTech are clear. However, there can be significant early costs in developing and deploying the system. Traditional sources of government support—appropriations and financing—might not be enough to support GovTech growth and scale. In this chapter, we look at potential future models by which governments might fund GovTech initiatives. The models under consideration include public-private partnerships (PPPs), impact investing, and crowdsourcing.

In preceding times, Government Technology projects were financed using a budget allocation. This means that part of the annual budget was earmarked for IT spending, including expenses for staff, hardware and software. There are, however, several disadvantages of such an approach. Firstly, the budget of any government is perennially claimed by competing priorities and political constraints which mean that funding for GovTech is always finite. Secondly, the budget allocation is always for the coming year only, so it is difficult to plan, and start, long-term IT projects.

In order to address these challenges, governments are increasingly implementing alternative funding models that utilize the expertise and resources of the private sector. Among those models is the public-private partnership (PPP), a specific project-based demonstration of Government 3.0, which involves cooperation between public authorities and private sector firms to conceive, build and maintain GovTech solutions. Within the PPP model, the private sector partner typically contributes the upfront capital investment and assumes some of the risks, while the public agency provides supervision to verify that the solution will be able to address the regulatory and legal requirements of the Government 3.0 project.

Public-private partnerships (PPPs) come in different types and shapes, including development partnerships, concessions, performance-based contracts and many more. Take a concession for example – the private sector is granted the license to take care of, provide services and generate revenue for a GovTech solution, in return for a share of the revenue generated by the solution in a fixed period. Such an arrangement gives incentives to the private sector to provide such a service in the highest standard, and to invest in the enhancement of the solution.

Another innovative fiscal prototype of GovTech is called impact investing. Impact investing aims to boost projects using private negotiable to job and have double hit: fiscal proceeds and good domestic or environmental results. Applied to GovTech, impact investors finance solutions to major public problems including education, climate, or health. Any form impact investing can appear in: it can be asset investments, loans or it can be social impact bonds.

Social impact bonds (SIBs), a venture capital financing, appear to be a particularly promising model for financing GovTech initiatives. Under a SIB arrangement; private investors provide the upfront capital to pay for the development of a GovTech solution and the government agency promises to repay the investors on the basis of specific social or environmental outcomes. In this way, SIBs can potentially align the incentives of a government agency and a private sector partner, and make sure that a GovTech solution is designed to achieve measurable impacts.

Another financing model that emerged is Crowdsourced funding. Crowdsourced financing is where online platforms are used to request small contributions from a large number of individuals and organizations. From the GovTech perspective, crowdsourced funding can be used for financing the development of open-source software, citizen-engagement platforms, or any other solutions that provide public goods. Crowdsourced funding can democratize the process of financing and actively engage citizens in the development process.

One example of crowdsourced funding success is Decidim. Created by the city of Barcelona to get its citizens to participate in their local governance, the project was initially financed by government subsidies and crowdsourced contributions from Barcelona residents and non-governmental organizations. Since going live in 2016, more than 100 organizations across the globe have adopted Decidim, which has led to more than 300,000 citizens participating in the decision-making process for their communities.

No matter what funding mechanism is employed, governments must also ensure that GovTech initiatives are financially sustainable in the long term. This necessitates careful planning and analysis to determine the cost and impact of each initiative and to create revenue models that can support ongoing operation and maintenance. Governments may have to explore new pricing models, such as subscription-based or usage-based pricing, to ensure that GovTech solutions are accessible and affordable to all citizens.

Overall, financing GovTech requires a variety of innovative funding models that exploit the resources and expertise of private industry. Public-private partnerships, impact investing, crowdsourcing of funding, and new methods can help address the problems associated with time-honored ways of funding government and support sustained growth and financing of GovTech. By careful assessment of costs and benefits and construction of sustainable revenue models, governments can make sure that GovTech solutions provide value to citizens and contribute to the digital transformation of public services.

# CHAPTER 7: SMART CITIES AND URBAN GOVERNANCE

The world is going through a rapid phase of urbanization. Due to this, there is immense pressure on cities to provide an efficient, sustainable, and liveable environment to their residents. GovTech plays an important role in meeting these challenges by building smart city projects. In this chapter, we will learn about smart cities - the concept, the role of emerging technologies in urban management, and the integration of smart technologies into urban planning and governance.

A smart city, at its essence, is a city that makes the most of digital technologies and data analytics to refine city operations, enrich public services, and improve the quality of life for its residents. Doing this entails deploying a suite of technologies, including the IoT, AI, and big data analytics, to gather and analyze real-time data about city operations and citizen behavior.

Urban infrastructure management is one of the most important use cases for smart city technologies. With IoT sensors and other monitoring devices deployed throughout a city, local officials can gain real-time visibility into the performance of critical infrastructure, such as transportation networks, energy grids, and water and waste management systems. This data can be used to allocate resources in a smarter way, proactively predict and prevent failures, and react more speedily to emergencies.

As a case in point, Barcelona has set up a smart water management system that melds IoT sensors to keep tabs on water level, quality, and flow rates throughout the city's network. It has contributed to Barcelona cutting water consumption by 25% and piloting its water governance operation. In comparison, Seoul has implemented a smart transportation system based on real-time traffic information and predictive analytics to optimize traffic flow and reduce congestion on city streets.

Besides improving transportation efficiency, smart technologies are applicable to critical aspects of public security and safety. By aggregating data from devices and conduits as diverse as surveillance cameras, social media feeds, and emergency response systems, cities gain a much deeper understanding of public safety threats and can respond much more effectively when those threats become incidents. AI-enhanced analytics help identify patterns and predict incidents before they occur, offering cities a chance to intervene before crime or other dangers can take hold, to the benefit of their citizens and their property.

New York City has recently put into place a smart public safety system that utilizes machine learning programs to analyze information from many different sources, such as 911 calls, social media feeds, and crime reports. This system allows the city to discover areas that are more likely to have public safety concerns and dispatch first responders accordingly. Months into use, the program has helped lower crime statistics across the Big Apple.

In addition to public safety and infrastructure, smart city technology has the ability to enhance the delivery of public services and increase citizen engagement. This can be done through things such as chatbots and virtual assistants that provide 24/7 access to information and services or mobile applications and online platforms that can be used for citizen involvement in decision-making.

Dubai has recently launched a smart city platform called DubaiNow. This system allows users to access more than 120 different government services through a single app on their mobile devices. The smart city has streamlined government services, minimizing red tape, and beam lining procedures, to make life easier for the city's inhabitants. DubaiNow has changed this equation and has revolutionized the transparency and accountability of these services in the process.

However, to fully realize the advantages of smart city technologies, cities must also incorporate these technologies into their broader urban planning and governance frameworks. The incorporation of smart city technologies into urban governance and planning requires a holistic approach that goes beyond just the technical aspects of smart city solutions to include the social, economic and environmental criteria by which smart city technologies should be guided and evaluated.

For instance, a smart city strategy with a focus on civic engagement and co-creation in smart solutions was developed by the City of Amsterdam. In numerous living labs and innovation districts, the city enabled the collaboration between citizens, businesses, and government agencies to develop and test innovative smart technologies and solutions.

In the same way, Singapore has instituted an expansive smart city infrastructure that is focused on sustainability and resilience. The scheme includes a strategy to support eco-friendly design, implement green transportation, promote renewable energy, and ultimately improve how resilient the city of Singapore is as the climate changes and the city is developed.

To sum up, smart cities represent a new "operating system" for urban governance in the 21st century. By exploiting major advances in information and communication technologies and data gathering and analysis, cities can optimize their operations, deliver high-quality public services, and improve the quality of life for their citizens. To capture and share these gains, however, cities must adopt a comprehensive approach—understanding the social, economic, and environmental dimensions of smart solutions and connecting these solutions to wider urban governance. In the next chapters, we will address some major challenges and dimensions of smart city construction. addressed issues of privacy and security, the correct public-private mix, the inclusion of all citizens in smart initiatives, the role of innovative procurement in these initiatives, and the need for new governing structures to manage them.

# CHAPTER 8: PUBLIC-PRIVATE PARTNERSHIPS AND INNOVATIONS

With governments worldwide turning to technology to deliver better public services and promote economic growth, GovTech innovation is increasingly shaped by collaboration within public-private partnerships (PPPs). This chapter examines how cooperation between governments and the private sector is critical, outlines models of successful public-private cooperation, and explains the development of thriving GovTech innovation ecosystems.

In essence, a PPP is an agreement between a government agency and a private company wherein the private company delivers a public product or service while at the same time absorbing large-scale financial, technical and operational liabilities. In the field of GovTech, PPPs can manifest themselves in many ways, from joint ventures and co-creation efforts to innovation challenges and accelerator programs.

One major benefit of PPPs is they empower governments to tap into the private sector's know-how, assets, and inventiveness. Whether joining forces with tech companies, start-ups, or other ideas factories, authorities can take advantage of the cleverest technologies and most promising approaches, which they don't necessarily have the capacity or expertise to construct alone. That, in turn, can accelerate GovTech's pace of innovation. It can also catalyze the birth of more compelling and potent public goods.

For instance, a few successful PPPs in the field of GovTech have been established by the Singaporean government. To tackle quandaries for the public sector, the Smart Nation and Digital Government Group (SNDGG) has linked government agencies, companies, and schools to create digital remedies. On top of that, SNDGG has launched a few pilot calls and incubators, known as the Open Innovation Platform and the Digital Services Accelerator. Both of these projects help to build and execute digital-friendly

GovTech solutions, and allows the public and private sectors to work together.

One more important upside to PPPs is they able to boost innovation and create an adapted framework for businesses, specifically startups and Small and medium-sized enterprises (SMEs). Like, PPPs give access to government data, infrastructure, and other resources that can diminish the startup cost for new business, and compensate for the inadequate resources. Also, It gives the chance to collaborate with others, and share new ideas for the business's growth and improvement.

One example is the British government. Several GovTech innovation programs and initiatives have been launched by the British government to encourage the growth of GovTech startups and SMEs. For instance, GovTech Catalyst offers grants and support for companies to develop innovative solutions to public sector challenges. Meanwhile, GovTech Innovation Network provides a platform through which startups and SMEs can network with government agencies and other partners, enabling them to collaborate and share knowledge.

In order to construct productive PPPs and nurture transformation in GovTech, governments also must generate a conducive environment that endorses collaboration, experimentation, and commensurate risk-taking. This could encompass designing exclusively dedicated innovation units or teams within the public management structure, providing capital or alternative resources for transformational projects, and constructing an open and candid cultural climate that encourages both networking and knowledge-sharing.

An example of making an enabling environment for development is to make a GovTech ecology by connecting private sector partners, Government organizations, academia and civil society organizations to team up on new initiatives in GovTech. There are unlimited approaches to making a GovTech ecology, from making physical recording centers and advancing cooperation center to building virtual GoTech systems and making joint effort stages for sharing information.

Estonia is a country that exemplifies GovTech's embrace. The Estonian government's e-residents center & briefing center as well as the Startup

Estonia program provide a variety of tools and mentorship to startups and technology innovators specializing in GovTech. Teaming with other nations to create public-private partnerships and other initiatives and examples like the X-road data exchange platform and the Estonian government's "e-residency" policy have helped Estonia develop a prospering tech environment as well.

Another way that governments can encourage innovation in GovTech is through the use of more flexible and agile procurement processes. Traditional government procurement processes can be very slow, overly complex, and overly risk-averse. This can make it difficult for startup companies and other innovators to get into the market. By using more streamlined, more flexible procurement processes, like innovation partnerships and challenge-based procurement, governments can create more opportunities for collaboration and experimentation with the private sector.

Henceforth, it can be concluded that the PPPs as well as innovation ecosystems are indispensable for bolstering the innovation of GovTech and facilitating the public services. It is rather necessary for Governments to team up with the private sector in order to allow innovation. Moreover, the government should focus on creating the conditions that induce innovation to happen. Additionally, it may be important that governments think about procurement processes that are more agile, and flexible. Further chapters are going to discuss some challenges and opportunities that are emerging behind innovation in GovTech and also PPPs. Also, it is important to discuss topics like intellectual property, risk, as well as skills and capability needs.

# CHAPTER 9: CYBERSECURITY AND DATA PRIVACY IN GOVTECH

With governments turning to digital services to dispense public services to citizens, making sure government data and systems are protected and confidential has grown vastly in importance. Cyber risks—to give just one example, hacking—could be ruinous for government operations and public trust, and digital pursuits also raise concerns about privacy and civil liberties. This chapter sets out the leading trials and best ways to build confidence in GovTech through cyber protection and data privacy.

An increasingly major headache for governments in the digital era is keeping ahead of the mounting complexity and regularity of cyberattacks. Avidly desired by cybercriminals, nation-states, and other malign actors, governments are founts of valuable data and sources of disruption for those looking to interfere with operations or shatter public confidence in governance institutions. A successful cyberattack against a government system can do grave harm, from monetary losses and reputational damage all the way to threats to national safety and public order.

To minimize these risks, governments must take a holistic, preventive approach to cyber security by implementing robust technical barriers such as firewalls, intrusion detection systems, and encryption, as well as developing sound governance policies and procedures to manage cyber risks. Governments must invest in ongoing education and awareness programs to ensure that employees understand the part they play in maintaining the security of government systems and information.

As an example, the Continuous Diagnostics and Mitigation (CDM) program is run by the United States Department of Homeland Security (DHS). Providing tools and services to federal agencies to recognize and defeat cybersecurity issues the report shows how over the course of time the program analyzes evolving risks and helps you respond to remediation. The

CDM has fourteen elements that help fight cybersecurity. Working with fifteen agents helps the CDM fight against the span of the attack from the Chairman and CFO, CISO, Program Management Office, Government, System Integrator/Solution Provider, Manufacturer/OEM, and through the chain of authority. The CDM does really well fight against large-scale threats and common Bernie attacks.

Besides implementing technical controls, the government should also establish comprehensive legal and regulatory frameworks for safeguarding user data and abiding by privacy rules and regulations. Enforcing a strong data governance policy is important, for instance, one that includes data classification and access controls. Furthermore, prioritizing that citizens are able to decide how data is collected, used, and shared and ensuring that citizens know and control what their data will be used for.

One example of a hyper-comprehensive legal framework that attempts to shield the data and individual privacy of citizens is the European Union's General Data Protection Regulation (GDPR). The GDPR empowers a complex regimen of rules for the non-aggregated collection, use, and dissemination of personal data by public entities and private sector entities, dovetailing in the hands of the citizen, the control of data thanks to provisions such as the right of access and the right of erasure (to be forgotten). Governments that benchmark themselves to GDPR and other privacy statutes will capture the trust of their citizens, assuring them that their data is being treated with reason and that it is transparent.

Another key to creating trust in GovTech is ensuring the transparency and accountability of government data practices. Governments will need to be open and clear about how they collect, use, and share citizen data, and also provide simple paths for citizens to access and control their data. This involves providing tools and mechanisms for data subjects' right of access requests, as well as creating independent oversight bodies to monitor government data practices and hold accountable organizations that breach the trust or misuse the data.

An example of an independent regulatory body that serves to enforce legal protections regarding personal data is the United Kingdom's Information Commissioner's Office or ICO. Known for impartiality, the ICO oversees data processes and acts as a mediator between UK citizens and government departments. Rulings carry weight because the ICO has the power to issue fines and deterrent penalties in response to a breach of data protection legislation. The ICO also encourages responsible practice, promoting transparency and accountability by fostering discussion, advising people and organizations, working with specialist partners, and making and promoting data privacy issues. So, who watches the watchmen? In the United Kingdom, citizens, campaigners, and private sector businesses rely on the ICO.

Governments can establish confidence in GovTech not only through legal and regulatory frameworks but also by embracing industry-leading secure software development and deployment practices. This involves using secure coding practices, running regular security audits and tests, and having all software and systems up-to-date with the latest security patches and updates.

For example, start with the Secure Software Development Framework (SSDF) and the Cybersecurity Framework (CSF), both given by the U.S. National Institute of Standards and Technology (NIST). NIST, along with many others, gives to the public heaps of formulated best practices and procedures. Utilizing these methods and methodologies will assist in the development of software and systems that are secure. Governments can design by inscription with security in mind.

In conclusion, establishing trust in GovTech through effective cybersecurity and data privacy measures is essential to the success of digital government initiatives. Taking a holistic and proactive approach to cybersecurity, creating strong legal and regulatory frameworks for data protection, ensuring transparency and accountability in data practices, as well as adopting secure software development best practices can help governments shield against the dangers of cyberattacks and data breaches, as well as earn the trust and confidence of citizens. In the next chapters, we will explore some of the cutting-edge technologies and techniques that governments can deploy to put in place effective cybersecurity and data privacy safeguards, including blockchain, encryption, and privacy-enhancing technologies for instance.

# CHAPTER 10: MEASURING SUCCESS OF GOVTECH PROGRAMS

Since governments are investing in GovTech to improve government service, increase operational efficiency, and drive innovation, determining whether these GovTech initiatives are successful and impactful becomes critical. Without defined metrics and evaluation processes, it becomes difficult to assess if GovTech projects are meeting their expectations, providing value for money, and delivering quantifiable benefits to citizens. This chapter addresses the important aspects and best practices of international standards for measuring GovTech initiatives' success, such as developing the key performance indicators (KPIs), data-driven evaluation, as well as benchmarking with international standards.

Defining key performance indicators (KPIs) that are clear and measurable is one of the initial steps taken to assess the success of GovTech projects. KPIs are measurements that are quantifiable and assist in monitoring progress toward goals and objectives. They may be useful for evaluating the performance of GovTech projects over time. When creating KPIs for GovTech projects, a variety of factors needs to be taken into consideration: for example, the specific goals of the project, the concerns and interests of stakeholders, and the availability and dependability of data.

Typically found within GovTech initiatives, some common KPIs might include measures of efficiency such as reduced processing times for government services, cost savings through automation and digitization, or increased productivity of government employees. Other KPIs might focus on measures of effectiveness such as improved citizen satisfaction with government services, increased access to services for underserved populations, or reduced error rates in government processes.

To illustrate, Estonia's government has created some KPIs for their e-Government projects which include such things as the portion of citizens that use the Internet government's services, the number of government operations that use digital signatures, and the cost savings of digitizing government operations. By using these KPIs over time the Estonian government can determine the outcomes of individual projects and flag problematic issues.

After determining the KPIs, there are three straightforward steps to be made: Develop a data-driven approach for evaluation and continuous improvement. Collect and analyze the data for GovTech initiatives performance. Use available tools such as data analytics, machine learning and data visualization to gain insights from the data. In this manner, the government could identify areas for improvement, optimize resources and make evidence-based decisions for future investments.

Take, for instance, the data-driven method the government of New Zealand devised to assess the influence of its digital government undertakings. The government instituted a group of data standards and protocols for reaping and distributing data through government agencies, as well as creating various analytic tools and dashboards to guide policymakers through understanding the performance of digital government services. Employing data to encourage continuous improvement, the government of New Zealand has managed to optimize its digital government activities and produce better outcomes for citizens.

Benchmarking against global best practices is another crucial factor in measuring the success of GovTech initiatives. By measuring the effectiveness of GovTech projects against those of other nations and regions, governments can see where their expertise is leading them and where they might not be keeping up. Authorities would also spot examples of best practices and lessons from other countries by benchmarking, which can be adapted and applied to their GovTech initiatives.

The United Nations E-Government Survey, for example, serves as a global measure of the development of e-government initiatives. It is based on a range of criteria, including online service delivery, telecommunications infrastructure, and human capital. Governments who take part in the survey can use it, and compare their performance with that of other countries, to identify where they make the most headway with their e-government projects and where they have their greatest shortcomings. This in turn helps them see how they can make progress.

Not only can governments compare themselves with the best globally, but they can also learn from peers in other countries and jurisdictions. In order to exchange know-how, ideas and learning from their own GovTech experiences, governments engage in international forums and networks similar to the OECD's Working Party on Digital Government or the Open Government Partnership.

To recap, it is crucial to evaluate the success of GovTech initiatives to ensure that these projects deliver value-for-money, improve public services, and drive government innovation. By setting up distinct and measurable KPIs; applying an evidence-based approach for evaluation and continuous improvement; connecting with international best practices; and engaging in peer learning and knowledge exchange, governments will gain essential insights on the outcomes of their GovTech initiatives and establish a logical trajectory to guide future investment. In the next few chapters, we will explore some of the key hurdles and pathways to replicating successful GovTech projects, and the role of GovTech projects in creating economic growth and enabling social progress.

# CHAPTER 11: EMERGING TRENDS AND LONG-TERM VISION

Governments are experiencing fundamental changes in the GovTech landscape around the world. They are adopting and incorporating technologies, Blockchain, AI, HealthTech, etc. into how they work and deliver services. The future of the operation of government is being shaped by newer technologies, citizen expectations adjusting, and shifting social, economic, and environmental priorities. In this chapter, we will scrutinize upcoming trends and technologies that will form a future round of GovTech along with a vision of a more efficient and citizen-centered government in the long run.

One of the most important emerging technologies that will shape the future of GovTech is artificial intelligence (AI). AI has the potential to transform, even disrupt, large swaths of government operations, starting with the automation of routine tasks and extending to decision-making, augmenting citizen engagement, and delivering personalized services. AI-powered chatbots and virtual agents provide people with round-the-clock access to government information and benefits and allow them to act on them. Machine learning algorithms can extract patterns and insights from government data to demonstrate or develop policies and programs.

Yet the government's implementation of AI also brings important ethical, and societal concerns, for example, the usage of AI that perpetuates biases and discrimination. The need for transparency and accountability in the use of AI for decision-making. Governments are going to have to create clear frameworks and guidelines for the responsible and ethical procurement and usage of AI in the public realm. Governments will also have to invest in the skills, and capabilities to adequately adapt manage and oversee AI.

Another game-changing technology on the horizon that will shape the GovTech of the future is blockchain, walking hand in hand with AI. A decentralized, distributed ledger technology, blockchain has the potential to revolutionize large parts of how government works – from secure record-keeping and identity management to open and efficient service delivery. Blockchain-based systems could create secure, indelible records of government transactions (think land titles or voting records), while also putting citizens far more in control of their own data.

However, the use of blockchain in government faces significant obstacles, such as industry collaboration and the technical integration of multiple blockchain platforms, as well as the difficulty of connecting new blockchain systems with existing legacy infrastructure. Ministries will need to modernize by investing in a research and development consortium to study technical obstacles and opportunities of Bitcoin technology.

Not only by these emerging technologies, the future of GovTech is likely to be shaped by many other factors. Some of those are, changing citizen expectations, and social, economic, and environmental priorities. Now citizens require more personalized, convenient and accessible government services, greater transparency and accountability in government decision-making. In the meantime, governments working under pressure to deal with important social and environmental challenges like inequality, climate change, and public health crises.

In order to tackle these challenges, governments need a more citizen-centric and data-driven approach to both service delivery and decision-making. This requires investing in user-centered design and agile development methods; building the data infrastructure and analytics capabilities necessary to uncover insights about citizens' needs and preferences; and fostering deeper collaboration and partnerships with the private sector, civil society, and academia to co-create innovative answers to complex public problems.

At its core, the future of GovTech is a more efficient, transparent, and citizen-centered government. But achieving this vision will require a complete change in how governments work and interact with citizens, and a willingness to adopt new technologies and new ways of working. It will require government services to be skilled, capable, and supported by the digital infrastructure needed to transform government.

To bring about this vision, governments need to take a comprehensive and strategic approach to GovTech that goes beyond simply adopting new technology. To achieve this vision, it will take developing clear roadmaps and blueprints for digital government transformation and investing in the human capital and organizational capabilities that will make change happen. But it also entails inclusively involving citizens and stakeholders in government service design and delivery and building trust and confidence in public sector use of technology.

In sum, the outlook for GovTech is a mixed bag of opportunities and challenges. On the one hand, emerging technologies like artificial intelligence and blockchain promise to revolutionize governmental operations and service delivery. On the other, a demand-side revolution driven by changing citizen expectations and societal, economic and environmental priorities beckons toward a reimagined digital government. To embrace this vision, governments must follow an enterprise-wide and future-minded approach that is centered on citizens and enabled by the skills, capabilities and infrastructure of the next stage in the digital revolution. Doing so will make government more efficient, transparent and citizen-centric, and will deliver better public services for the 21st century and beyond.

# CHAPTER 12: EXAMPLES OF GOVTECH IMPLEMENTATIONS

In order to offer practical insights and ideas to government leaders and stakeholders, five successful GovTech applications from around the world are presented in this chapter. The case studies dive into different sectors and regions to prove that GovTech can be applied to a diverse area of workings. Each case study also goes into the perks of the initiative as well as the things that have been learned.

1. A Comprehensive Digital Government Ecosystem: Estonia's e-Estonia

    - How Estonia transformed from a post-Soviet state to a thriving digital society
    - What you need to know: X-Road, e-ID, and all the other components of the ecosystem
    - Proven results: efficiency, transparency, citizen satisfaction, and more
    - Key considerations for starting a digital government transformation

2. Singapore's "Smart Nation" Vision: Harnessing GovTech for Urban Innovation

    - Singapore's "Smart Nation" - vision and its goals
    - Showcasing select GovTech projects e.g. the National Digital Identity (NDI), Smart Urban Mobility solutions, and the Smart Nation Sensor Platform

- Outputs in terms of better urban management, service delivery, and citizen engagement
- Sharing Singapore's strategy in public-private partnerships and citizen co-creation in GovTech development.

3. The Government Digital Service in the UK (GDS): The User's Drive to Improve Public Service

    - GDS as a driver of the digital revolution on behalf of the government
    - During the session, the speakers will cover the key impacts of major digital services like GOV.UK, the Digital Marketplace and the Government as a Platform Approach (GaaP)
    - Thanks to these services, the speakers will also highlight the benefits realized from channel shift, cost savings, user experience improvements, and trust in public service.
    - Finally, the speakers will take us through their lessons on user-centric, agile digital service development and the adoption of public services for a world gone digital.

4. India's Aadhaar Program: Leveraging Digital Identity for Inclusive Service Delivery

    - Aadhaar program of India, the world's major biometric identity system.
    - The numerous uses of the Aadhaar this include, Economic add-on, Public welfare, Health applications
    - The operation and reason achieved add-on to these services, decrease in method of the services, de-escalate in waste of money, Efficiency
    - Lessons Chosen on Privacy. Security, Stakeholder Engagement in large - scale digital identity projects

5. RealMe in New Zealand: A Digital Identity Solution for Efficient Online Service Access

- RealMe platform in New Zealand as a secure digital identity solution to access certain government services
- Emphasize the advantages of RealMe, such as making it easier for users to use it, maximizing protection, and increasing reliance on online transactions and ratios
- Details of performance levels achieved in terms of user adoption, earnings efficiency and consumer satisfaction
- Description of New Zealand mechanisms of public-private collaboration and connectivity for digital identity management.

Through the presentation of these case studies, the objective of this chapter is to offer readers a more comprehensive understanding of how GovTech may be properly implemented within various contexts. Every case study will offer practical insights and suggestions that leading governmental officials and stakeholders may personalize and implement in their own GovTech initiative(s).

To sum up, this chapter will distill four key lessons from these cases before concluding. Stressing the vital role played by leadership commitment, user-centric design, public-private collaboration, and continuous improvement in driving successful GovTech implementations, this brief synthesis of synthesis will enable readers to see more clearly the main features of a positive landscape. Armed with this outline of threats and opportunities, they will be better placed to begin charting a course through the complex path of GovTech adoption within their own organizations and jurisdictions.

# ACKNOWLEDGEMENT

In the creation of this seminal series, I have had the distinct privilege of drawing upon the invaluable experiences, insights, and expertise generously shared by a distinguished global network of esteemed partners and accomplished friends. Their direct and indirect contributions have been instrumental, and it is with profound gratitude that I acknowledge the indelible influence they have had on this work.

Kanth Krishnan: Managing Director at Accenture, has been a beacon of inspiration with his incisive insights and visionary leadership in technology services. His profound depth of knowledge and innovative approach have significantly enriched the content of this book.

As Managing Director at Newmark, Jeff Pappas has provided critical perspectives on the dynamic global real estate market landscape. His unparalleled expertise has contributed to a deeper understanding of the business environments explored herein.

Haitao Qi, Chairman of Devott Research and Advisory, has provided exceptionally enlightening perspectives on technology innovations and market trends, especially in the Asian context.

Formerly leading Outsourcing and Managed Services at PwC, Charles Aird's comprehensive knowledge and strategic foresight in outsourcing services have greatly contributed to my understanding of this critical business function.

Mike Beares: Founder and Board Chairman of Clutch.co, has been instrumental in shaping my views on business connectivity through his entrepreneurial spirit and dedication to bridging businesses with the optimal service providers.

It has been my great privilege to learn from and collaborate with these distinguished individuals and institutions operating at the leading edge of our industry. Any merits of this book stem directly from the exceptional global network of friends and partners upon whom I rely. Any faults or shortcomings are solely my own.

Last but not least, the unwavering understanding and support of my beloved wife, Biyu, has been an inspiration to this professional endeavor. The intensive writing workload harkened back to my doctoral dissertation at Yale a quarter-century ago. She remains the driving force behind my career growth and personal fulfillment.

# ABOUT THE AUTHOR

## Stephan S. Sunn

Stephan Sunn is the Executive Partner at Sanford Black Advisory, a preeminent global business and investment consultancy. In this capacity, he collaborates with industry leaders to advise companies worldwide on growth strategy, marketing/sales, innovation monetization, partnerships, and mergers & acquisitions. Over the past two decades, Mr. Sunn has consulted on sourcing provider selection for more than 30 international corporations and over 20 investment and M&A deals in the technology services, digital technologies, and global outsourcing sectors.

Mr. Sunn possesses particular expertise in empowering private enterprises to accelerate growth and enhance value creation through engagement with governments and technology parks. He holds a leadership position with Devott Co., China's largest private research firm focused on the IT, software, and technology services industries. Additionally, he serves as a Director at the China IT and Outsourcing Association. His clients span Fortune 500 companies, state-owned enterprises, technology parks, SMBs, and startups in both developed and emerging markets.

A graduate of the University of Science and Technology of China (USTC) with a Bachelor of Science degree, and Yale University with a Master of Science and Ph.D., Mr. Sunn frequently shares his insights and research as a speaker at global conferences and events. He is a prolific author and an accomplished presenter for his projects and clients around the world.

# BOOKS BY THIS AUTHOR

## Competing For The Growth

This book serves as a guidebook for city planners, economic development professionals, tech park builders, and public officials who aim to create thriving innovation communities that attract global trade and stimulate investments. It offers a structured path that begins with intangible factors like vision setting and partnership alignment and extends to pilots and full-blown magnet programs.

The book provides real-life instructions to help put these ideas into practice, including effective strategies for attracting rapidly growing businesses and talent, creating a setting that promotes innovation and entrepreneurship, fostering a competitive and appealing business climate, and building a globally recognized brand and reputation.

The author emphasizes that cities and tech parks must play to their strengths and assets to compete and win in the global arena. The race for relevance is on, and the window of opportunity to determine the outcome is closing. Cities and companies have what they need to succeed, and with the options, relationships, and guidance provided in this book, city managers and tech park authorities can make the decisions necessary to lead their communities to success in the world investment and trade arena.

## Searching The New Profits

In the face of global market turbulence and domestic uncertainties, American small and medium-sized businesses (SMBs) and startups have significant growth opportunities in emerging markets. However, these markets also present unique challenges. This handbook provides a semi-analytical and semi-prescriptive approach to help American SMBs and entrepreneurs succeed in these rapidly expanding markets. Conversely, governments, technology parks, and corporations in emerging countries can utilize this book to learn how to collaborate with U.S. companies in their markets to serve their customers effectively.

The book covers essential themes such as researching and identifying matching markets, choosing the appropriate market entry mode, local marketing and sales tactics, effective risk management, establishing an active and reputable presence in the local market, ensuring full legal compliance, avoiding political involvement, talent search and retention, and balancing standardization and localization. The final chapter shares valuable lessons from decades of business practices, acknowledging that readers may have different perspectives on these topics. Expanding knowledge through diverse viewpoints is beneficial for U.S. SMB and startup leaders. Despite the challenges, penetrating foreign markets can be highly profitable, and U.S. enterprises have a reasonable chance of success by capitalizing on the vast potential of these rapidly growing territories.

## Cracking The Winning Codes

This book serves as a comprehensive guide for international technology and outsourcing companies seeking to enter and succeed in the highly competitive U.S. market. It emphasizes the importance of adapting to the unique American business culture, which values innovation, diversity, relationships, customer-centricity, and results-oriented management. The guide highlights the need to navigate the complex U.S. regulatory landscape, including federal and state laws, as well as key legislations such as FCPA, SOX, and HIPAA.

The book covers essential topics such as understanding American business culture, complying with legal requirements, developing effective marketing strategies, employing successful sales techniques, addressing cultural differences, and managing risks associated with entering a new market. Additionally, it encourages the use of innovative tactics to differentiate from competitors and gain market share.

A special section titled "The Lessons" shares the author's personal experiences and insights, providing practical execution tips that focus on solution-oriented approaches, leveraging referrals and testimonials, managing communication costs, delivering higher quality than promised, and investing in proven local sales leaders.

By adhering to the core principles of understanding buyer preferences, continuous innovation, human capital development, risk management, customer-centricity, and resilient operations, global providers can successfully navigate and thrive in the lucrative U.S. market.

# Win More Businesses

In the digital age, businesses must navigate the complex landscape of Marketing Technology (Martech) and Sales Technology (Salestech) to stay competitive and drive growth. "Win More Deals in Global Markets" provides a comprehensive guide for leveraging these technologies to enhance customer experiences, streamline processes, and boost revenue across international markets. The book explores the convergence of marketing, sales, and technology, emphasizing the importance of data-driven decision-making and cross-functional collaboration. It offers strategies for overcoming challenges in digital transformation, such as resistance to change and skills gaps, while also addressing the unique considerations of global expansion and localization.

The authors predict future trends in Martech and Salestech, including the increasing role of AI, personalization, and emerging technologies like AR/VR and voice interfaces. Through real-world success stories from global brands like Coca-Cola, Sephora, and Airbnb, readers gain valuable insights into harnessing the power of these technologies for business success. This book serves as an essential resource for executives and professionals seeking to navigate the digital ecosystem and drive growth in the international marketplace.

# Renovations Or Revolutions

The book "Renovation or Revolution? Impacts of Latest AI on BPO and Contact-centers Industries" provides an in-depth exploration of the transformative potential of artificial intelligence (AI) within the business process outsourcing (BPO) and contact center industries. It emphasizes the importance of early adoption, customization, and localization of AI solutions to gain a competitive edge in the global marketplace. The book highlights the evolving role of human agents, who will focus on complex problem-solving and relationship-building, while AI handles routine tasks. It also discusses the development of AI expertise within organizations and the ethical considerations surrounding AI implementation.

The authors present a roadmap for incorporating AI, underlining the need for a clear vision, employee training, and continuous improvement. Looking ahead, the book envisions a future of collaborative human-AI partnerships, hyper-personalization, and proactive customer engagement. It stresses that embracing AI is crucial for BPO and contact center companies to achieve sustainable growth and remain competitive in the international arena. The book serves as a comprehensive guide for executives navigating the AI revolution in the global business services industry.

## Risky Reefs In The Ocean Of Global Markets

This book provides a comprehensive roadmap for emerging market companies venturing into global expansion. It highlights common pitfalls across strategic planning, finance, operations, human resources, marketing, technology, legal/ethics, and risk management. The book emphasizes thorough market research, cultural adaptation, local partnerships, brand building, innovation investment, and long-term vision.
As the global landscape evolves, it anticipates trends like digitization, sustainability integration, and talent acquisition challenges. The book provides corporate decision-makers with insights and best practices to navigate complexities, mitigate risks, and foster sustainable growth while driving innovation and progress internationally.

## The AI Revolution In B2B Marketing And Sales

This professional guidance provides a comprehensive playbook for leveraging artificial intelligence (AI) to drive measurable results in B2B marketing and sales strategies. With insights from real-world case studies spanning diverse industries and business sizes, it explores AI's transformative impact on understanding the AI-empowered buyer, delivering personalized omnichannel experiences, boosting sales productivity, and optimizing operations.

The book offers a strategic framework for successful AI implementation, covering data readiness, talent acquisition, governance, and ethical considerations. Globally applicable principles foster human-AI collaboration, enabling organizations worldwide to harness AI's potential ethically and profitably in the B2B domain.

www.ingramcontent.com/pod-product-compliance
Lightning Source LLC
Chambersburg PA
CBHW072054230526
45479CB00010B/1052